How To Analyze People By Looking At Their Body Language

How To Reading People And Decode Nonverbal Communication In Society

Robert Tower

Table Of Contents

If you love listening to audiobooks on the go, I have great news for you. You can download the audiobook version of this Author for FREE just by signing up for a FREE 30-day Audible trial! See below for more details!

Audible Trial Benefits

As an audible customer, you will receive the below benefits with your 30-day free trial:

- FREE audible book copy of this book
- After the trial, you will get 1 credit each month to use on any audiobook
- Your credits automatically roll over to the next month if you don't use them
- Choose from Audible's 200,000 + titles
- Listen anywhere with the Audible app across multiple devices
- Make easy, no-hassle exchanges of any audiobook you don't love
- Keep your audiobooks forever, even if you cancel your membership
- And much more!

Click the links or scan your QR Code below to get started!

For Audible US

For Audible UK

For Audible FR

For Audible DE

Introduction

Body language gives a hint about the emotional state of the person. For this reason, exhibiting the right body language and understanding body language accurately can improve communication as well as enhance life chances. Some aspects of life that need body language are parenting, teaching, talking therapy, and intimacy. Against this backdrop, this book offers the much-needed understanding and application of body language reading competencies for a novice and professional communicator.

Analyzing or reading your audience helps you gain information that can be built upon for establishing a common ground between them and to make your speech even more relatable and persuasive. For instance, if you are presenting a network marketing opportunity to people and their body language reveals that they are all ambitious people who love to lead a good life but who are thoroughly dissatisfied with their current jobs.

It is easy to influence, persuade and inspire people when you know how to read their thoughts and feelings. It is also easier to establish your authority, credibility, and integrity as a leader when you know how to read people's reactions to your actions.

People will be in a position to select the right leaders simply by observing their body language for clues related to deception, integrity, empathy, and power. By observing the person's verbal and non-verbal communication patterns, you'll be able to gauge if they'd indeed be the right leaders.

Your ability to read someone is not always about what you can see. At times, it is also about what you feel when you are around them. Trust in your gut feeling. Many people ignore this. Gut feelings are a primal instinct that protects you from something or someone you are not comfortable with. When speaking to a liar, they might spin tales that have you wondering whether they are true or not. If you have a shred of doubt about it, you are likely right about them.

The best way to go about life is to be open to possibilities. Not all possibilities might be amazing, but in human interaction, it is always safe to expect the unexpected. Considering the different types of liars out there, you have to protect your space. Recognize that some people are beyond help, but suggest professional help for those who can benefit from it. It is painful when you have to distance yourself from people you love because you cannot trust them to tell you the truth.

The ability to analyze people is an often undervalued and underestimated skill. But almost anyone can gain a huge advantage if they took the time to study and understand why people act the way they do. By learning to analyze people, you get the advantage of knowing that person's feelings, emotions, and attitude even before the person utters a single word.

Moreover, the ability to analyze people helps you understand what the other person is going through. With this understanding, you can become empathetic (if the situation calls for empathy) and know what to do to make the person feel comfortable.

Chapter 1: Body Language

What does it mean to be able to read someone? What does it take to influence the way others read you? When reading, others are mentioned, at least in this book, what's meant is a sizing up of several unspoken factors, either consciously or subconsciously.

A sizing-up usually consists of rapidly taking in details about someone's personal information and personality type based on body language, facial expression, appearance, and gesticulation. Surprisingly (or perhaps not so surprising), what you say with words only accounts for a small portion of someone's opinion about you. It was recently revealed in studies that body language, facial expression, and appearance all ranked higher in the forming of someone's opinion about another individual, so much so that these silent communications made up more than half of the basis for the opinion — speaking only accounted for about 15% of the basis for the opinion.

Whether we like it or not, appearance is most frequently the initial basis for an opinion to form. We're a very visual society, and we've come to know and trust the micro-information we gather within just seconds of seeing someone. Of course, that's not to say the first impression of someone is always entirely accurate. We're all aware of stories that illustrate the risks of judging someone based on their appearance. A beggar could be a prince under the outward appearance. The new employee could be the boss undercover. But this doesn't change the fact that we, as humans, process, visual information about someone the moment we see them. By and large, it's not even a conscious behavior; we're doing it unconsciously. A visual assessment like this has helped to keep us safe for thousands of years, so it's built into us.

But there is a difference between processing information to make educated guesses about someone, and consciously using that information to form a judgment of someone's value. This is where real-life morals try to teach us about making impulsive judgments about someone; condemning them or idolizing them, based on their appearance. A dangerous practice indeed, and if this is your approach, it's only a matter of time before that backfires on you, too.

Though we may observe a person's hairstyle, clothing, shoes, or car to make relatively innocuous determinations about them, we do not need to weigh a person's value based upon these things. For example, a scruffy, unkempt look with dirty clothes and worn shoes may provide us with a rough estimation that this individual may not have the means to look good, or the individual may not put too much value on appearance him or herself. Both of these pieces of information can instantly help you to make a connection and build a rapport with someone, better than without. You may find as you connect, that there's an entirely different reason for the appearance, but it doesn't matter much, because you have not judged a person's value by these details. You've only used these details to form some sort of an idea about who someone is, and because you have virtually no value connected to any of it, it's easy for you to adapt your perception of someone as you go along.

Other unspoken cues continue to inform you and help to form a determination as you go along through the interaction. The way someone stands, whether they make eye contact, whether they use their hands and body to gesticulate or whether they remain calm and still. The movements of their eyebrows and their lips. All of these little details are being processed by us consciously or subconsciously and helping to create an idea of who someone is and what they're all about.

Reading the unspoken body language is a highly effective skill, but you can even read into someone's spoken communication for more unspoken clues. By paying attention to the tones and inflections someone uses, you can determine how they truly feel about a situation regardless of what they report to feel. It's often the words people don't say that reveal the most.

The best way to learn about reading others accurately, and broadcasting yourself deliberately, is to understand basic human behavior. By acquainting yourself more closely with our basic human instincts and tendencies, you'll be able to pick up twice as much information in an interactive as you used to. You'll begin to notice it in all the interactions you have, and you'll become more aware of when you do it, too. This alone will make you a much better persuasive communicator, but we can go further than that.

In this section, you'll gain clarity on which common basic concerns drive us as human beings, and how the persuasive individual can use this information to influence a situation by either reading it and responding to it, or by portraying it as a subtle, unspoken, manipulation. We'll focus for the most part on body language, gestures, and expressions, how to read them, and how to use them. Cognizant of your broadcasting, and theirs. You don't have to do anything with this information just yet necessarily. Training yourself to look and listen for it and recognize it is sufficient for now.

The Basics of Body Language

Think back to one of the most recent interactions you've had. Perhaps this was a situation at work, or the store, or at a recent event. Take a moment to think back to that scene. Remember where you were, who was there, what was being discussed or done; think of the details of the moment. Try to see yourself there again. Now consider the posture you were standing with and the posture, others around you were holding. Ask yourself if anyone had their arms crossed. Were they looking toward the door?

Each of these small details is revealing information about you or others around you. These details can be used to move the interaction along positively and beneficially, or they can clue you into someone else's true intentions.

Posture is a common way for us to gauge someone's self-confidence and self-image. In a typical case, a slouching posture can be indicative of someone with a lower level of self-confidence and self-worth than someone who stands tall. However, a stance can be too aggressive or too close to the personal space of another, and you will be perceived as overbearing. Posture is one of the first pieces of body language we perceive to either consciously or subconsciously draw inferences from it about the person.

We pick up information about posture as soon as we get a visual of someone, but there is another tactic we can use discreetly to help you identify some basics about a prospect. The tactic is to look for certain clues that tell you whether your prospect is a visual, auditory, or kinesthetic sort of individual.

Though there are plenty of similarities amongst us in human behavior, one of the ways we differ from one another is by how we best digest information from the world around us. We use our five senses to register information, but one of our senses stands out as dominant against the others. This is typically indicative of the type of person you are and how you better digest details about your surroundings. There are three dominant senses we use to take in and retain information: visual, auditory, and kinesthetic. Though most of us use all of these senses for absorbing information

The Sight-Based Person

This personality type is the most common amongst us, making up about 75% of people. Concepts and memories are mainly stored in the mind as visual images and pictures. When they speak, visual people tend to use language that pertains to vision to express themselves. For example, a visual person might say:

- "I'd like to get your perspective."
- "You're a sight for sore eyes."
- "That's not the vision I had in mind."

Physically, the visual person will generally stand with an upright, front-facing posture. This person is typically well-dressed and put together because they tend to be more concerned with their visual appearance.

When a visual individual is experiencing stress, it tends to be gathered and held in the shoulder area. This might look like the shoulders rounding and pulling up toward the ears, or it might look like the shoulders, pulling back and forcing the spinal area to stiffen. That's not to say all individuals with visible tension in their shoulders are visual people, but it's quite common, and it would be a smart piece of information to intuit, even if you end up changing your mind later based on more information about the person.

When visual people are trying to remember something, they tend to look upwards. This causes them to develop wrinkles in the center of the forehead. These individuals tend to have thin lips instead of full lips, which is subconsciously indicative of a responsible, practical, personality type. This individual is comfortable making regular eye contact, and they start to feel uneasy if others will not make eye contact with them. For this personality, eye contact is an important part of building trust in the rapport, and it's an indication to them that you're paying attention as they speak.

The Sound-Based Person

This personality type accounts for about 20% of the people we interact with. Concepts and memories are primarily stored in the mind as sounds, noises, melodies, and quotes. When they speak, auditory people tend to use language that pertains to hearing and sound to express themselves. For example, an auditory person might say:

- "I want to voice my concerns."
- "Let's wait until we get the word."
- "A bell went off in my mind when I saw him."

Physically, the auditory personality type may not be as well-dressed or as concerned with appearance as the visual personality. This is because the visual representation of themselves to others is less important to them than the information; they share through talking, sound, and voice.

The auditory individual doesn't enjoy eye contact as much as visual people. In situations where eye contact would be normal, the auditory person may avoid it. Contrary to the way it may appear to some, this is not a sign of disrespect or disinterest. The auditory person looks down, looks at relevant papers, or moves a pen around on paper, making a subtle sound. This is the auditory person concentrating on what you're saying. Eye contact would be more uncomfortable and therefore, distracting. Rather than be distracted, the auditory individual is looking somewhere arbitrary to focus on the sound of what you're saying.

This is the type of personality that clicks their pen, taps their foot, or drums quietly on the table. This is the most effective way for these individuals to digest, process, and store information. They are creating a memorable and meaningful experience with the information to be saved in mind by sound patterns which makes the information easier to recall in the future.

The Touch-Based Person

This personality type is the hugger. They account for about 5% of the individuals we interact with. This is the type of individual who likes to get to know you by sharing personal space with you and touching in various ways. Like the visual and the auditory personalities, the kinesthetic person will speak in ways that use a touch- and feeling-based vocabulary. They might use phrases like:

• "I like to be hands-on."
• "Let's put a pin in it for now."

- "I have a bad feeling about this."

This individual wants to be near others and wants to get a sense of a person's "vibe" by spending time with them in the same (usually small) space. They tend to be the "touchy-feely" kind of person who prefers to build a rapport based on physicality and feelings. They love to connect with others, even in platonic ways, with a touch on the arm or shoulder. You'll always find the kinesthetic person dressed for comfort.

If you interact with kinesthetic people, or you are a kinesthetic personality yourself, it's important to keep a few things in mind for the most successful interactions. Remember that while kinesthetic people like to touch to communicate, not everyone else does. Some people are very put off by physical contact. For some individuals, it's distracting to have their personal space disrupted, so they prefer not to hug or make affectionate gestures. It's important to respect both sides of the interaction and come to a sort of subconscious compromise.

If you're the kinesthetic person interacting with primarily visual and auditory people, acknowledge that the majority of people are not kinesthetic communicators; yours is a small category of individuals. While there are plenty of visual and auditory personalities that still appreciate hugs and the like, it's still not necessarily the way they best absorb information. When you're building a rapport, a touch can be a good thing, but if you intend to educate or persuade an individual, you will want to use an approach that matches their personality type for the best results.

If you're a kinesthetic person testing the waters to see if others are receptive to touch, you can start slow and see how it goes, but you must pay attention and take notice of the subtle cues from the individual. An overbearing kinesthetic approach is the fastest to get shut down because instincts for protection subconsciously come up. Depending on the situation, it can be nice to start with light and casual forms of contact, such as a handshake or an elbow-to-elbow bump as an accent to a conversation piece. As you build a rapport, you will be able to determine if you can communicate with this individual more tactically.

If you're not a kinesthetic personality and you don't like to touch, you don't have to. But understand that most people do use the contact of some sort for basic communication so be prepared. If you're okay with a handshake, you can extend your hand a second before others, to subconsciously set a boundary of your personal space. If your hand is very extended from yourself, others will get the message to respect the space around your body. This establishes a point of contact for others but comfortably signals a boundary.

Gestures and Expressions

With a solid grasp on how we instinctively react, and which factors play a part in our reactions, you are capable of an overall assessment of someone (or yourself). Looking for clues of whether they are more likely to be visual, auditory, or kinesthetic will give you more insight and leverage for your interaction. But there's another layer deeper we can go. Next, let's take a look at the most commonly used subconscious expressions and gestures and what they mean.

Facial Expressions

An easy way to interpret someone's comfort level by looking at their faces is to pay attention to his or her eyebrows. Eyebrows can be very revealing about the level of relaxation for others around you. Eyebrows that relax to the outside of the brow are generally comfortable in the interaction. A raised eyebrow is often a sign of interest or skepticism. To determine which, try to look for other clues in gesture and expression. Both raised eyebrows are a sign that an individual is feeling surprised, fear, or worry.

The side glance is a subconscious movement that also reveals when an individual is nervous or uncomfortable. The eyes looking to the side are searching subconsciously for an exit from the interaction.

Lips can be a little more difficult to read, and the takeaway can be rather vague, but typically those with fuller, larger lips tend to be more free-spirited, childlike, and even immature. Those with thinner lips are perceived as more responsible and mature. Though we might not mean to, we do read into the shape of peoples' lips. Next time you're in a crowd, take note of whether individuals have thin or full lips and whether that trait seems to match up with other inferences you may be able to draw out from speech and body language.

Nodding is an interesting trait to observe because we (at least in the Western world) tend to use nods to mean a variety of things from mundane to sinister. The trick here, like eye contact, is in the context. A person could be nodding to signal you to hurry along with your conversation subconsciously. Or, they could be nodding because they want to express concern and care for your emotions, or agreement with your statements. Look for other behaviors that might help you to refine your assessment.

People tend to touch their jaw or chin with a hand when they're making decisions in their minds. However, there's a difference between doing this seriously, and doing this behavior to appear as though a decision is being made when one is not. There is a long history of this gesture being linked to contemplation or decision-making. From Shakespeare to Bugs Bunny, people also make this gesture when they want you to think they are making a decision or consideration. For this reason, you should pay extra close attention to where the person's eyes are pointed when they do this. If a genuine decision is being made, the individual's eyes will likely be pointed down and to one side when they touch their jaw or chin. If this same gesture is made, but the person's eyes are looking straight ahead, or at you, the consideration is likely a false one.

Stance and feet are also an important communication tool to take note of. The distance between your feet, the direction they're pointing, and whether they're crossed can all be indications of how open a person is in conversation. If a person's feet are pointed toward you and a shoulder distance apart, they are likely more willing to share information with you and trust you. If the feet are pointing toward a door, close together, or crossed, the individual is guarded and may have some emotional walls up. If the feet are placed more than a shoulder distance apart, the stance is an aggressive one.

Crossed arms or legs are a strong subconscious sign that an individual is closed off to the interaction This may be out of an exaggerated need to protect oneself in general, but it could also be a sign that they are specifically untrusting of the person to whom they are conversing.

Now it's time to start paying attention. You're aware of human reactions that drive us, and you're aware of factors that play a role in how we react. It's time to start analyzing people for practice. When you're at a meeting, an event, or in line at the grocery store, examine the body language of those around you. Can you tell who communicates best with visual vocabulary and who the hugger is? Consider the body language you're giving off in these same places. Is it accurate? Is it the image you wish to be sent?

For the next seven days, make these observations about yourself and others in at least one scenario. In a notebook or on your phone, record the date and the interaction or place. Then record your observations. The goal is to become a keen observer and sharpen your people-reading skills over the seven days. At the end of seven days, look back over your observations, and see if they've become more observant and more accurate each day.

It's recommended that you continue this practice for a few weeks at least. This will help to program you to look for information on body language automatically, and it will help you to sharpen the image of yourself you want to broadcast. As you continue the assignment, remember to go back and analyze your entries to gauge how well you're progressing.

Chapter 2: Posture and Body Orientation

While we have touched on a few here and there, knowing how people communicate with various movements of their body parts will deliver a lot about them. You will decipher more about a person's personality and character, as well as their intention through how they move around. It includes how they move parts of their body around, and how they generally place themselves.

Body language has two major parts: Kinesics and proxemics. Kinesics is how someone moves their body or parts of their body. Proxemics, on the other hand, is the distance between bodies and what they signify. When you become a skilled observer, you will have a reasonably accurate glimpse into what someone is thinking. That way, you can then manipulate them better.

Kinesics

Kinesics refers to the movements of body parts, which someone can use to reinforce what they are saying, or can reveal what someone is trying to hide. This way, you gain an advantage that you can use to read their minds and make your move to persuade and influence them.

They include

Body Posture - closed/open arms, slumped shoulders, etc.

Body posture is basically, how someone places their body. In body language, there are two types; closed and open body postures.

A closed body posture will typically mean that the person has his hands folded across his chest. They will cross their legs and face away from the person talking to them. Some people have slumped shoulders and curved backs.

This closed body posture often communicates either that the person is uncomfortable or not interested in what you are saying. When someone has slumped shoulders and a curved back, they may be struggling with confidence, or have a lot going through their mind and feel the weight weighing them down.

An open body posture, on the other hand, communicates interest and a desire to be approached and engaged. This posture will mean that the person is welcome to a conversation and will be receptive to your desire to speak with them.

When someone has an upright standing posture, they are likely more confident and happier. These people may be optimistic.

Mirroring

Mirroring is the act where you match your body movements with the other person so that you create a synchronic situation that helps establish a bond between people. Mirroring, also called mimicry helps build trust, even when the person you are mirroring does not realize it.

While it sounds creepy, when you do it naturally, and with the right intention - to understand the other person better, it will help you read into what the other person is not saying.

Mirroring can take many forms. If the person you are talking to folds their arms, for example, it could be a sign that they are getting uncomfortable. However, you can copy them so that they become more at ease as they take it that they can trust you.

Alternatively, when they lean forward, it shows that they are interested in the conversation. Lean forward too. You could also lean forward as a cue for the other person to lean in. Leaning helps, you learn more about them to that, you can then read their mind and learn how you can persuade them.

You can mimic with words too. Take a keen interest in the words that the other person frequently. Then, begin to use them sparingly through the conversation. Subconsciously, the other person will start to settle in your presence. This ease gives you room to analyze them and know how you can then approach them to persuade them of your point.

Facial Expressions

Facial expressions are other very revealing body movements. Dr. Paul Ekman, a researcher, found that we use seven different micro-expressions that reveal the bigger picture; surprise, fear, disgust, anger, contempt, sadness, and happiness. These micro-expressions determined how to read well if someone was faking.

A genuine smile, for example, should involve various muscles on the face; cheeks, lips, and eye muscles. A genuine smile will spread across the whole look. Keep note of that when someone smiles at you.

Proxemics

Proxemics is the study of how we relate to personal space. The thing with proxemics is that it is different from cultures and varies from individual to individual.

However, there is little that we can learn from proxemics.

Close Distance - Interest

There is a close distance called the close range. We have this kind of distance from people that we are close with and trust. Often, entering into this distance with someone you are not close with is disturbing and creepy in many cultures and with many people.

So, to avoid turning off the other person, keep a safe distance. Ensure that you are close enough, but not too close to make them uncomfortable and close out to your interactions.

Someone might also get close to you if they are interested in you. The person might not get too close to you, but they will get close enough to you to pass a message. If a person is trying to catch your attention, for example, they will get into your personal space but not get into the close distance. However, as we have learned, context is vital. Use this measure with other indicators, as someone might stand close to you because that is the appropriate distance in their culture, or that is just how they view space.

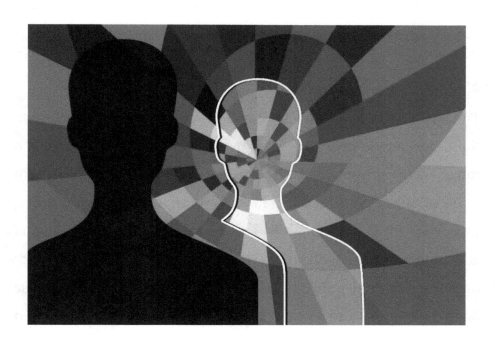

Social Distance - Impersonal/Formal

Social Distance is the distance we maintain with people such as business associates, people we are professional around. We often use social distance for co-workers with who we are not well acquainted or business associates.

The distance also refers to tilt. If one person sits in a position where they appear to look down on the other person, it may mean that they want to come across as authoritative.

Pubic Distance - Respectability

This distance happens in a situation where you cannot get close to the other person because of the many limiting factors. At such a range, arm movement and gestures become critical. When in public, make a point of using head movement to pass your point, especially when you speak to a crowd. These body movements allow them to bond with you despite the distance. Look at some of the most admired public speakers. You will notice that they use hand movements and gestures a lot, as well as head movement and exaggerated facial expressions.

Our body language speaks in ways that we should take time to understand. But, as we have said, always use them in context for better analysis of the other person.

Chapter 3: How to Recognize Who is Lying to You

A lie can be defined as an assertion that is believed to be forced to simply deceive somebody. Lies involve a variety of interpersonal and psychological functions for the people who use them. People use lies for various reasons which are, at most times, best known to them only. It is believed that every human being can lie. Multiple types of research have suggested that on an average day, people tell one or two lies a day. Some surveys have suggested that 96 percent of people admitted to telling a lie at times while 60 percent of a research study done in the United States claimed that they do not lie at all. However, the researchers found at least half of that number were lying. However, scientists say that there are ways in which one can easily spot a lie or be able to know when somebody is lying to you. Lies can be intended to protect someone while others are very serious like covering up a crime done. People do not know what ways they can use to detect a lie, and most of them end up telling themselves that they can easily detect a lie. You can easily recognize a lie by noting down the nonverbal cues that people use like for example, a liar cannot look you directly in the eye; however, researchers have proven that this might not necessarily work. In 2006, Bond and De Pablo found out that only

54 percent of people were able to detect a lie in a laboratory setting. Investigators also do not find it easy to detect a lie and can easily be fooled into believing what is not. Most people believe that trusting your instincts always is the best way to avoid being fooled.

Gesture

This is a form of nonverbal communication where body actions tend to speak or communicate particular messages. Gestures include the movement of hands, feet, face, and other body parts. Gestures enable one to communicate non-verbally to express a variety of feelings and thoughts. For example, people can communicate none verbally when they are in trouble and need somebody's help. The gesturing process comes from the brain which is used by speech and sign language. It is believed that language came from manual gestures that were being sued by the Homo sapiens. This theory is known as the gestural theory that was brought about by the renowned philosopher Abbe de Condillac in the 18th century. However, the use of gestures can be a way to note when somebody is lying to you. Some people find it hard to control their body motions when telling a lie. That is why gestures are used to detect when somebody is lying to you. Different body expressions will tell you when a person is lying.

The Mouth Cover

This gesture has been at most times used in childhood. A person lying to you will cover their mouth when trying to prevent themselves from saying the deceitful words. Most people do not entirely cover their mouths but use just a few fingers covering the lips. Other people may try to fake a cough to be able to get a chance to cover their mouths, which by the way, does not make any difference whether they cover it fully or partly. However, this gesture needs to be carefully examined before concluding that the person is lying. If the person covering the mouth is the one talking then it is most likely that they are the ones lying and if the one covering the mouth is the one listening then this might be a show that they are carefully listening to what is being said and might be probably thinking that you are not sincere with them. People who can note this behavior cannot be easily fooled or manipulated or controlled in any way. The liar will always be afraid of approaching the person since they are afraid that their intentions will easily be noticed. This reduces the rate at which people use others to their advantage thereby influencing the community ethically.

The Nose Touch

Most people that lie tend to always touch their noses while talking. After letting go of their mouth, they tend to touch their nose and try to fake that they are itching. It is almost instant to note when it is just a normal nose itch or when someone is trying to use it to hide a lie. A normal itch can be relieved quickly by just a simple scratch, but if someone keeps on scratching and touching their noses, meaning that they are lying.

The Eye Rub

The brain tends to use the eye trick as a way of hiding deceit. People who lie tend to rub their eyes to hide the clear show from their eyes that they are lying. A lot of people find it difficult to maintain eye contact when they are lying, and they tend to shy off every time they look at the person they are lying to. They, therefore, rub their eyes to hide from the fact that they are lying. People say that the eyes tend to create a sign of doubt to the person you are talking to. This is why most people rub their eyes to hide this sign.it is said that men do it very vigorously while women do it gently without having to hurt themselves much. Being able to recognize this gesture will help the community and society at large to be able to fight off liars.

The Ear Grab

When a person is lying, they tend to touch and play around with their ear lobe as they talk. This makes one feel a bit more comfortable while telling a lie and also trying to block themselves from hearing the words that they are saying. Children tend to cover their eyes when they hear something they suspect is a lie, and they do not want to hear it.

Neck Scratch and Other Body Parts

Adults who lie tend to use their index finger for scratching their neck just below their ear lobe. This is done a few times, showing that the person is lying. A person who is lying tends to also put a finger in the mouth when they feel they are under a lot of pressure. Lying creates a very uncomfortable state for people and they, therefore, are unable to control their feelings around the people they are lying to.

Change in Breathing and the Collar Pull

This gesture art was first discovered by Desmond Morris when he noticed that there is always a tingling sensation in the facial and neck tissues, which causes one to rub or scratch that place a couple of times. The increased blood pressure brings about the sweating of the palms and at times even under the armpits. This makes you short of breath when you start suspecting that the person you are deceiving might not be believing you. This is called a reflex action.

The Position Change of the Head

People do tend to make quick and sudden head movements after they have been given a direct question or query, they are likely to be lying about something. They will either retract the head, or it will face downwards or even be tilted to one side before they answer the question you had asked them.

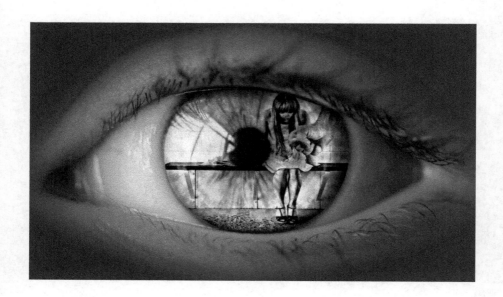

Feet Shuffling, Holding a Stare and Standing Still

People who are not moving at all when you engage in a conversation with them should be a call for concern. It is normal that when you two people converse, there is a movement of the body in a relaxed way, but if the other person is very rigid and seems relaxed in a very extraordinary way could show that probably there is something very off about that person. The shuffling of the feet is brought about by being nervous and uncomfortable. It could also show that the person eagerly wants to leave the conversation as soon as possible. Looking at a person's feet and their movements tell you a lot about what that person is saying. It is renowned that most people are unable to maintain eye contact when lying; however, some other people don't move an eye or blink when they are lying to you in a quest to completely pull you off with their lie and manipulation. Liars tend to use a cold stare when trying to intimidate and control you.

The above-explained gestures are seen in a lot of people that try to manipulate people or lie to them to get what they want. However, it is good if you all have these skills that will help you in identifying people that play around with your mind or may want to use yours to your advantage. Most people who lie will lack words to say since all their tactics have been revealed and learned by everyone.

Facial Expressions

The facial expressions that a person makes tell you a lot, whether they are lying or not. Lies to you become obvious when you can learn these different cues in a conversation. All that goes around someone's face shows either dishonesty or honesty in a conversation. The following are the facial expressions that may tell you that a person is lying.

The Eyes

The eyes are what most people use to note whether the other person is telling the truth or they are just lying. The eyes create a link to both imagination and memory. Imagination is often seen as a good thing when one is creating a lie. This is because one can imagine situations in their head and also try to figure out the reaction of that person after they hear the lie.it is said that when a person looks up to and to the left after being asked a question, they are usually trying to recall some information where the memory comes in. this act is often told to be the truth. When someone looks up and to the right, they are utilizing their imagination or in other words, fabricating information to give to you. This is taken as a lie. After asking a question pay close attention to the person's eyes and which direction they move. The eyebrows also tend to raise when they are telling the truth and tend to blink or close their eyes a lot to steal time for them to rethink their lie and make sure that their story is kept intact without having to betray themselves through the eyes. Most people that lie also tend to avoid eye contact with the person they are talking to. When forced to make eye contact, they often feel uncomfortable and may even fall short of words making the other person know that they were trying to lie to them.

Blushing

When a person is telling a lie, they tend to often blush. They become nervous thereby creating an increase in the body temperature, especially around the face area. Blood tends to flow in the cheeks thereby causing the liar to blush or shy away. Although blushing can be stimulated by a couple of many other things, it is almost certain for a liar to blush. This might be a good way also to know when somebody is blushing.

Smiling

A person that lies while smiling does not have a lot of facial expressions like the flickering of the eyes to show that their smile is real. However, liars smile with "dead eyes" that do not brighten up their faces. A real smile has a great effect on the eyes and tends to cause the eyes to either become big or small. This is because more muscles are used in becoming happy rather than forced demands. A liar always has a fake smile whereby the truth of their lie is revealed by their eyes yet again. Being able to distinguish between a real and fake smile will help you in distinguishing between a person who is telling the truth and one who is lying.

Microexpressions

Facial expressions that easily come and go quickly serve as the best indicators that a person might be lying. These expressions are known as micro-expressions. These expressions prove to be great lie detectors and reveal the raw truth. These expressions also reveal if there is something wrong since it is hard to hide these expressions. However, it is good to note that not all micro-expressions reveal that a person is lying this is why it is highly advised that you be trained on how best to note and differentiate these feelings. Before concluding that the person you are questioning is lying it is advisable that you first check on the circumstance and situation at hand.

Speech

The way a person speaks while in front of you can tell a lot in terms of truth and lies. Liars tend to repeat themselves a lot while speaking because they are not sure of what they are saying and are struggling to convince themselves of their lies. A person who is lying to you tends to speak in a very fast way which enables them to bring out the lies in a very fast and consistent way. They are often left wondering whether the lie they told would be believable causing them to have an increase in heartbeats. Liars tend to add more or extra details to their stories to be able to convince their listeners that what they are saying is true. They take brief moments to rehearse or go over the answers they had rehearsed before to ensure that they do not make any mistake that will make their listeners doubt them. They at times become defensive about their answers and also tend to play the victim if they think their lie is not going as they had planned. However, the liar does not stand a chance if the person telling lies has expertise in understanding and knowing when a person is lying to them or when trying to create a lie.

The Direction of the Eyes

People who may not be telling the truth may tend to look to the left to construct or create imagery in their heads. Looking up and to the right is considered to be an effort to try and remember something that happened which is true as compared to looking up and to the left which is considered as trying to create a lie through imagination. However, this might be a little bit confusing for those people that are left-handed. Left-handed people tend to do the opposite of this theory, they look up and to the right when trying to create a lie and look up and to the left when trying to remember some events that took part in the past. The left side of a left-handed person is considered true while the right side is considered to be a lie.

Voice Change

Gregg McCrary, a retired federal bureau of investigations criminal profiler, stated that a person's voice might change abruptly when they tell a lie. This strategy works by first noting their speech patterns by asking simple questions for example, where they live. By this one can monitor the various changes in the speaking tones when they are faced with a more challenging question. A person who learns this art can easily tell when a person is telling or trying to create a lie.

The facial expressions explain above clearly show that people must learn these arts to be able to deal with people in society who love manipulating others. These people tend to confuse people by lying to them and making these lies true so that they can get away with their lies. A person who is not able to identify such kinds of people is at a higher risk of getting blackmailed by these people and making you do want they want to do, for example, commit a crime for them.

Chapter 4: Mastering Your Emotions to Identify Manipulation

I'm fine. That's the most common lie told. Deception and manipulation have become so commonplace today that everyone has been either a victim or a culprit at some point. You've either been lied to, or you've told lies. You've been deceived, or you've done the deceiving. You've been manipulated, or you're the manipulator. Still, not all lies are intended to deceive you. For example, when someone tells you 'Yeah, I'm fine, don't worry about it and they're not fine, it could be just their way of preventing you from asking more questions because they don't necessarily feel like talking about it just yet.

The signs of deception are there, once you know what you're looking for. One indicator (aside from body language) that deception could be taking place is when people start sidetracking the questions posed with long-winded, unnecessary explanations. Manipulators, liars, and deceivers are all around you, everywhere that you go. Sometimes, they could exist within your social circle, even within a family.

As different as they may be as individuals, there are certain things that manipulators have in common with each other, and that is the fact that they're sneaky, deceptive, underhanded, and will resort to using any tactic if it means they get what they want at the end of the day. They care little about your feelings or anyone else's for that matter, even the people they love, and they have no qualms about using your emotions against you. When you've got very little control over your emotions, you become an easy target. The only thing that matters is them is their agenda and getting what they want.

Lying is the oldest form of manipulation in existence. Anyone who's trying to manipulate or take advantage of another will resort to this tactic for their benefit, even thriving and taking pleasure in the knowledge that they've managed to pull the wool over your eyes. A skilled liar and manipulator know how to work this angle ever so subtly that unless you are adept at reading body language, you won't know what's happening until it's too late and you've either been lied to or deceived. People lie to take advantage of others. They manipulate to conceal their real motives. They lie to put themselves one step ahead of the competition.

Deception and manipulation are all around you. Even at work. An employee who was concerned about their job might approach the boss and ask about the possibility of being laid off or fired. The boss may try to hide what's going for fear of jeopardizing the work that still needs to be done by deceiving the employee into believing that nothing is going on. Assuring the employee that everything is alright, and there's nothing to worry about. All the while knowing it's a lie. A colleague who has been eyeing that same promotion you are might withhold potential information so that they could put themselves ahead of you. Parents who want their kids to do what they want could resort to manipulative tactics to get them to follow the rules.

Manipulators could be highly emotional individuals, prone to dramatic or even hysterical outbursts when they want things done their way. If you're not the master of your own emotions, you could easily get swept up at the moment and become just as overly emotional. So emotional in fact that it starts to cloud your judgment and stops you from thinking clearly. The worst part is that they play on your emotions by pretending to be your friend, gaining your trust to gather information which they could use against you in the future.

Why Do I Need to Learn to Master My Emotions?

Because without control over your emotions, you have very little control over a lot of other aspects of your life. You react inappropriately when your emotions are not regulated, which leads you to do or say the wrong thing. You get worked up over the smallest issues, making it difficult for others to be around you. You become volatile and prone to mood swings, which reflects poorly on your behavior and who you are as a person. Once you've been labeled as someone who is "overly emotional", people start avoiding you and make excuses to not be in your company.

Most importantly, not being in control over your emotions makes you an easy target. A manipulator on the prowl will easily know which buttons to push that gets you riled up enough and play on your emotions to coerce you into doing things you ordinarily would not have done. If you don't learn to master your emotions, then your emotions (and the manipulators around you) will become *your master* instead.

Indicators That Signal You're Being Manipulated

We're always trying to influence each other in some way. Encouraging friends to try a new product because you like it. Sharing ideas and trying to get others to see things from your point of view and why your approach should be the one to follow. Sharing views and video content across social media to sway others into agreeing with you. Leaders, managers, supervisors, and bosses influence people under their leadership, encouraging them to work towards a common goal. Advertisers and marketers try to influence customers into buying products and services through the various ads and marketing campaigns that they roll out. If influence takes place all the time, when does it cross the line from influence into manipulation? What sets manipulation apart from persuasion or influence? Isn't manipulation, persuasion, or influence essentially the same thing? Where you're trying to get one, or several other people to go along or agree with you?

Manipulation, persuasion, and influence *are* the same but called different names. There is one, defining quality that separates manipulation from the other two, and that is *the intention*. Manipulation is cunning and ruthless, and it always results in one person being exploited or taken advantage of. Persuasion and influence are neither cunning nor ruthless. Manipulation is carried out for selfish reasons that only benefit the one who is doing the manipulating.

Manipulators force others into doing their bidding through pressure and threats. The intention that lies behind your actions is what separates persuasion and influence from manipulation. Good intentions with a genuine desire to create a situation that benefits the other party is what persuasion and influence encompass. If you intend to do good, that's persuasion. If you're honest from the very beginning about what you're trying to do, that's persuasion. If you can say wholeheartedly that you have the other person's best interest at heart, that's persuasion.

Manipulators care for no one except themselves. There is only one agenda on their mind, and it only focuses on them, their needs, their desires, and what's in it for them. If they get what they want, they don't care who gets hurt along the way. If they must step on your toes to reach the finish line, they'll do it. If they must stab you in the back to get to the top, they'll do it. They don't care about the consequences of their actions, they only care about getting their way.

Manipulation is all around you, and you could be an unknowing victim even as you're reading this. Your first clue that you might be a victim of manipulation is when you sense that something isn't quite right with a certain relationship that you have. You can't quite put your finger on it, but being around that person never makes you feel good. Even among friends and family, instead of feeling happy after spending time with them, you find yourself even more stressed, frustrated, or confused than when you first started.

Or perhaps it could be that co-worker at work who always seems to sucker you into doing their bidding, even when you tried to resist in the beginning. For some reason, you feel *guilty* about not helping them, even though you had every right to say no because you've got your workload to deal with. These could be signs you were in the presence of a manipulator.

Manipulation takes place in several ways, and it could be anywhere from dealing with a bossy, demanding person to being in a relationship with an abusive partner. Some manipulative tendencies are easier to spot, while others are carefully disguised to make it seem like this kind of behavior is "normal". If you sense something amiss, go with your gut instinct and look out for the warning signs below that signal you might be a victim of manipulation:

Always Your Fault - A classic sign of manipulation is when no matter what you say or do, somehow, it's always your fault. Even when it's not. Even when you haven't done anything, you're the one to blame? How does that work? Well, the manipulator is an expert at twisting and turning the facts to suit the situation. You happen to be an easy target. That one manipulative friend who always has an excuse for their bad behavior or poor judgment, the one that always makes you the scapegoat, that's not a friend. That's a manipulator. I wouldn't have done it if you agreed it was a bad idea. Thanks a lot, now look what you've done! Why didn't you stop me? The classic sign of a manipulative "friend" is when somehow, you're always in the mix and the one made to feel like you're in the wrong.

Forced Agreeability - Do you often feel forced into doing things you don't want to do because the person making the request makes you feel bad about yourself if you say no? Being constantly made to feel guilty, pressured, or forced into agreeing, especially if it's by the same person, is not normal behavior. That's manipulative behavior, and they're playing on your guilt emotion to their advantage. What's worse, if you feel afraid to say no, that's a red flag that something about this relationship is not right. Not at all. You should never be made to feel like you're bullied or pressured into agreeing, but if you don't learn to master your emotions, manipulators will easily take advantage of this by making you feel as guilty as possible.

Insecurity - You were so sure of yourself and your decision 5 minutes ago. Then you were around that one family member, friend, or colleague and suddenly, you're not so sure anymore. 5 minutes ago, you were confident and sure, but now that same decision fills you with doubt, causing you to question your judgment. All after that one encounter. Does this sound familiar? If it does, you might have to face the fact that is family, friend or colleague is a manipulator. Spend enough time with them and they'll make you feel unworthy like you're a complete failure and nothing you can do will ever be right. Talk to them about any thought, idea, or opinion and they'll find a way to twist and turn it, making it seem like a terrible idea.

Chapter 5: Signs Of Confidence And Lack Of Confidence

Signs of Confidence

One of the things that separate the weak from the strong is confidence. Confidence is an important characteristic that is vital for one's survival in this world. To forge ahead in life, stay ahead of the competition and make your voice heard. Confidence is an important skill that you cannot do without. This explains why if a candidate goes for a job interview, no matter how smart, knowledgeable, experienced and skilled they are, failure to show forth confidence during the interview will bring down the chances of getting a job. A confident candidate, even though not as brilliant and experienced, will easily outshine the other candidate.

In the same manner, your chances of getting your dream girl increase if you carry yourself with confidence rather than a gloomy and timid aura with low self-esteem.

Self-confidence is pretty vital in every area of your life. There are signs to show that you have self-confidence. Hence, you can imbibe some of these tips to raise your confidence.

1.   You Do Not Hesitate

In other words, confident people are assertive. They know what they want and how to get it. They are not dissuaded by the ideas and opinions of others as long as they know they are on the right path. They are different from people who cannot make a decision, and they keep changing their minds without a clear-cut direction on what they are doing.

2.   You Are Comfortable in Yourself

This is pretty obvious. Confident people do not seek to be like another person in a bid to appear cool or acceptable to others. They know their strengths and weaknesses and have come to terms with who they are.

They are confident in their ability to go after what they want and achieve it. They do not need to be approved by anyone or fake their personality for approval.

3.   You Are Not Easily Influenced

How easy it is for people to influence and manipulate you is a big pointer to your level of confidence. Resisting influence is different from being proud. Rather, it is about being aware of who you are, what you want, and whose advice you take. It is taking responsibility for your life and being able to make the needed decision.

4.   You Don't Need Approval from Others

Many people, in a bid to know whether they are right, seek the validation of others. This validation is important for them to feel good and know that their choices are right. Genuine confidence, on the other hand, does not need any validation since there is an inner witness that validates you.

As a result of this, you have peace with all your life choices and decisions, and you do not need anyone to make you feel good about them.

5.   You Listen More than You Speak

Behind the mask of bragging is insecurity. A truly confident person does not see the need to brag. They are already at peace with themselves, their feelings, and their thoughts. They are after your thoughts.

As a result, they give people the freedom to express themselves. Since they are already at peace with their skills and knowledge, they seek to know more. Hence, they allow others to speak by listening more.

6.   They Allow Others to Shine

No matter their input in any task, no matter if they did the bulk of the work, no matter if they were responsible for the success of others, they allow others to shine. Recognition does not matter to confident people.

They are content enough in the success of their team and their effort. Hence, external validation, acknowledgment, or glory does not matter to them. Their satisfaction comes from within. As a result, they are neither afraid nor selfish to allow others to take the spotlight.

7.   They Do Not Put Others Down

Behind the gossip, comparisons, and bringing others down is desperation to be like others and even to appear better than them. Truly confident people, on the other hand, always seek to be better than themselves. They strive to accomplish the ideal person they hope to be, not anyone else.

8.   They Own Up to Their Mistakes

With confidence comes sincerity and honesty. This is why it is easy for confident people to let people know about their screw-ups. They don't mind being cautious for others to learn. A confident person sees nothing wrong in "looking bad" once in a while.

Signs of Lack of Confidence

Lack of confidence is something you cannot hide, and this will be reflected in many ways discussed below:

1. Inability to Accept Compliment

Someone with a healthy confidence level accepts compliments with a "thank you." They do not go about making excuses and giving a reason for why they do not merit it. They accept any positive review of themselves.

Such attention might make them uncomfortable, yet a major sign of confidence is being comfortable in accepting praise from others. They might even see themselves as lucky rather than taking the glory for anything.

2. Lack of Eye Contact

It is usually quite difficult for people with a low confidence level to meet the gaze of others. The eyes, they say, are the window to the soul. People with a low level of confidence are worried that eye-to-eye contact will make you see right through them, which will make you see their flaws. As a result, they are downright uncomfortable meeting the gaze of others.

3.   Unnecessary Apologies

Apologizing when you have done nothing wrong is a classic sign of a low confidence level. They will apologize for something they didn't do. When they hand over their project output to you, they will apologize for its quality even before you have had a chance to check it.

Their lack of confidence in themselves makes them accept a scolding; hence, in a bid to avoid it, they give preemptive self-criticism.

4.   Being Indecisive

People with a low level of confidence will not be able to make simple decisions. Since they are plagued with self-doubt, simple decisions like what to say will be difficult. They have a fear of criticism since they know that making a wrong decision will warrant scolding.

In a bid to avoid this criticism or scolding, they pass on the opportunity to make any decision, or they turn the responsibility to others. They do not see themselves as capable of making the right decision as the fear hinders them from weighing the pros and cons of their decision objectively. Hence, they believe others should make the decision and take the fall should something go wrong.

5.   The Need to Explain

Someone without enough self-confidence will be compelled to explain their actions, whether right or not. No one is above mistakes, but people with low levels of confidence will feel the urge to give reasons for their actions. Even if they are successful, there is the urge to explain their choices and decisions.

6.   Blaming Others

The inability to accept and own up for your mistakes is a classic sign of a lack of confidence. In a bid to avoid taking the fall, they put the responsibility off themselves and pass it to the person they are complaining about. This is a classic sign of lack of confidence in that they do not see themselves strong enough to handle any heat that comes as a result of their mistake.

7.   Making Excuses

Someone without enough confidence will be quick to make an excuse for any shortcomings and criticism. A confident person, on the other hand, will likely listen to the criticism and decide whether it is helpful or not rather than passing it off immediately with an excuse.

People who are quick to make excuses for their actions do so because of the fear of being seen as worthless person. Hence, they see the excuse as an escape route to manage and keep their ego intact.

8.   Need for Acceptance

People with a low level of self-confidence do need the attention of others to feel good about themselves and their choices. They need the acceptance of others to feel worthy. Hence, the lack of this acceptance could be frustrating as it affects their confidence level. A confident person, on the other hand, has realized that not everyone will approve of their choices. They know that all they need as validation is from within. This makes them good with their decision, whether others see sense in it or not.

9.   Their Body Language Reveals It

Consider a person with a cheerful countenance walking with their head straight and their hands-free. Consider another person bent, with hands in the pockets. It is evident which of these two is confident. There are postures you take that reveal a lack of confidence. Hence, confidence is revealed by the way you carry yourself.

Chapter 6: Know Yourself Well To Understand Others

How well do you understand your body language? How well do you know of your reaction to factors, both internal and external?

Learning how to read another person's body language down to the finer details would be useless if you would not know how you come across yourself. Your attempt to persuade another person to your side would be inconsequential if you did not know how you are presenting yourself. You need to be aware of; the pitch of your voice, what are your arms saying, your eyes, and your facial expressions. Whatever you put out, is what determines how others pick up your message.

How to Know Yourself Better

Identify Your Personality

To be able to work on your general body posture, you first need to identify your personality. If you want to be more charismatic and are introverted, jumping right into trying to appear more outgoing might come off as you faking it. If you are extroverted and want to be charismatic, you need to know if you exude confidence or talk a lot.

Identifying your personality is critical as it gives you a gauge of what you desire and what you do not. If you are not very outgoing, then becoming outgoing just for the sake of it will work against you.

Body Posture

Stand upright and try to be more relaxed if you are going to want to come off as confident and approachable. Unnatural slouched shoulders make you look less confident and unapproachable. When you speak to someone lean in a little to show that, you are interested in what they are saying. If you can help it, do not cross your arms. Let the other person get comfortable with you, and trust you.

Be Flexible When Communicating

When you put a point across, and the other person does not seem to be receptive to the idea, learn how to change your body language. You could change the style of delivery to convince them to see your point of view too.

Practice Facial Expression

Facial expression will often have a way of backing or taking away the punch from what we are saying. Practice this on the mirror in different scenarios. Look at how you express yourself when you are trying to convince, or when you are flirting, or when you are trying to be more confident. Refine them accordingly so that you have a better chance of convincing the other person of your point of view. Learning how to read others is an art, so is learning how to understand yourself. To read others better, you need to read yourself almost flawlessly.

Intention

Your intention guides how you align your body language to what you are saying. This book teaches you to persuade. Therefore, you need to learn how your body language will help you convince another person.

When speaking to someone else, for example, you can nod your head subtlety as you make your point. Take a tab of their language and see how you can then use it to create a bond between the two of you so that they can grow to trust you.

Gestures

Using gestures when you make a point makes you come off as more charismatic and thus, will make you more trustworthy. Make use of your arms when you make a point. Use it especially, to bring out your energy and emotions to the issue you are raising. Gestures make people grow more comfortable around you.

Once you understand the above, you will find that getting to manipulate and influence people becomes more manageable, since you use your knowledge of yourself to read them and act accordingly. You will read people well this way and analyze them with startling accuracy once you know yourself well.

Chapter 7: Techniques, Tips, and Tricks to Speed Read Anyone

Now that we have had a chance to look at speed reading and what it is all about, it is time to pay attention to some of the ways that we can use speed reading to help us pick out the right target, work with the target correctly, and ensure that we are going to be able to pick the right technique to use against them.

Speed reading isn't necessarily as hard to do as it may seem. We often will speed read those around us without even noticing. If you have ever ignored or stayed away from someone because you felt the anger and frustration from them, and you didn't want to get into it with them, then this is an example of how you used speed reading to see how that person was doing, and then protect yourself by avoiding them.

As a manipulator though, you need to take this up a notch. Your goal is to catch on to some of the things that may be hidden, the things that the target and others around you don't necessarily want to share, but they end up doing so through their emotions, their actions, and your intuition. This is how you start to know your target and can make it easier to manipulate them. Some of the tips and techniques that you can focus on when it comes to speed reading your target, as well as speed reading some of the other people around you in all situations include:

Observe their Body language

The best way to work on speed reading another person is to pay attention to their body language. We touched on a few of the different things that you can watch out for when it comes to body language, but it is surprising how much information we can gather from someone else simply because we can observe the body language that they share.

Many people are not aware of the information that they end up sharing with others through their body language. They may assume that they are keeping things secret and hiding the inner workings of their mind from others. But a skilled manipulator will be able to see right through this and can catch the changes in voice tone, hand gestures, and even slight movements of the eyes to see what the target may be hiding, and what they mean when they say certain things.

Using the body language tools that we talked about earlier in this guidebook can help you to get this done. You will find that you will be able to read all of the little nuances that are presented with the body language and catch onto things that the target never really thought would get out, much fewer things they didn't want to reveal to you. This makes the job of manipulating your target the way that you want.

Listen to What your Intuition is Telling You

Your intuition is going to be super important when it comes to working against a target. Sometimes you will find someone who may seem like the perfect target, but there is something about them that sends your intuition through the roof and you don't feel comfortable with it. It is much better to wait for the right target, and listen to your intuition than to jump in and end up with too much work and trouble in the process.

Your intuition is like your subconscious telling you that something is now quite right in a processor in a person. We may not be able to pinpoint exactly what seems off to us but something isn't right and we don't feel comfortable with it. While other people may choose to ignore these signals and concentrate on getting things done, going forward even when their intuition is telling them to slow down.

Often our intuition is going to sense things, and know things before our conscious mind can catch up. And if we learn how to follow it and listen to the warning that it is giving to us, we are going to see that some action is not the best for us to take. It may seem a bit silly and like we are missing out on a lot of opportunities out there, but in reality, it could save us a lot of work and effort in the process.

Now, your intuition can also come into play to help you avoid getting manipulated. Just because you are using dark manipulation and dark psychology does not mean that someone else is not trying to do the same thing to you or that you are immune to some of the effects. Assuming this is going to land you in a lot of issues and can make it difficult to get the results that you want with your manipulation. How are you supposed to manipulate someone else and get them to do what you want if someone is already working on and manipulating you at the same time?

Listening to your intuition will not only help you to speed read another person and pick out the right target to use for your needs but will ensure that no one else is going to take advantage of you. You will be able to sense when someone else is trying to use these tactics on you, especially when you are using them at the same time. So, listen to that intuition so that you can keep yourself safe in the process as well.

The final thing that we are going to take a look at here is the idea of the emotional energy from the target. This emotional energy is going to tell you a lot about that person and can help you to understand what they are feeling and how they are going to act. When someone is happier and upbeat, this usually means they have had a good day or some good news, and they are more likely to want to help you out and do a favor. But when they are down and not feeling the best, they will likely be more closed off and harder to work with to get to do what you want.

Reading the emotions of the other person is going to make a big difference. Just because someone is going through some motions and knows how to control their body language doesn't mean that the emotions aren't going to tell you something about them. And you can use this to your advantage.

Let's say that you notice someone is in a pretty good mood. They are beaming and can't keep the smile off their face. They are standing tall with good posture, and maybe even bouncing a bit because they are so excited or in such a good mood overall. They may even talk a bit faster because they just can't keep it all in. These people have just found out some good news or are just having an amazing day.

Because they feel this way, they are more likely to feel generous and want to help others out. maybe they want to spread out the love and happiness so they will help out with the favors that you want. At the very least, they are not going to be concerned about a little inconvenience when you ask for a favor because they are already in a good mood. This is the perfect time for you to attack. You will be able to come in and ask for any kind of favor that you would like and it is likely the target will be willing and happy to do it.

Now, someone in a different mood may not react in the same manner. They may not want to open up, if they are in a bad mood, they will think the world is out to get them and will be more frustrated when you do ask for a favor. Or they will get sad and want to close up to you. If you ask this kind of person for a favor or try to manipulate them, it is going to end up badly for you. The target is going to get upset, will refuse you, and it could end the relationship and the bond that you are trying to create.

This doesn't mean that you have to give up hope. But it helps you to stop and think about whether this is the right time to ask or favor or try to manipulate your target. But that doesn't mean that they won't be ready to manipulate later on. It simply means that you need to do some work first. Maybe instead of walking away or even trying to ask for a favor when your target is in a bad mood, you can stop and see if you can get them in a better mood.

This may not open the door for your work right now, but it will later. The target is going to be thankful that you took the time to help them feel better about the situation, and they are going to remember that you made them laugh, made their day better, and helped them to get out of a sour mood. And later, when they are in a better mood and you need some help, they will be more willing to help you out without any issues along the way.

Speed reading people is a unique thing that you can add to your dark psychology plan and it takes some of your dark manipulations to the next level. This method is going to ensure that you know the person you want to target and will make it easier for you to find the right target, figure out how to manipulate them, and even learn when is the right time to start some of the manipulations.

Conclusion

Whether you want to figure out the personality of a potentially big client during a negotiation or the characteristics of the hot new prospective date you have your eyes on, this book is a handy resource for helping you read others effectively. If there's a single largest skill that spells success in today's world, it is the ability to read people.

This allows you to mold your message according to the personality of the other person to accomplish optimally beneficial communication.

The next step is to use the book and apply it in your daily life in small, gradual ways to begin with. Start by observing people at the airport or doctor's clinic when you have some time at hand. The interest will quickly catch on, and you'll find yourself taking a deep interest in reading and analyzing people.

Our smiles are one of the most powerful tools we've been given. You can turn any situation from bad to good just by turning up the corners of your mouth. Some people feel as though if they don't have straight teeth or smiles that are bright white, they aren't worth anything. Even those that don't have all their teeth can have much more beautiful smiles than someone that's spent thousands on dental work.

A smile isn't just about what teeth you're showing. It's a way to engage another person. Studies have proven that most people will smile if someone else smiles at them first. If they do smile, they'll end up having a better mood overall. It can seem weird, but simply smiling can lift someone's spirits. Next time you are feeling particularly down, smile. It sounds so silly, but it might work. Smile over and over again, and even though it might not turn your mood around, it will certainly help to at least temporarily lift your spirits. Now you know how to read people like a book. Your life will become so much easier now that you have finished this book and learned the critical life skill of reading other people.

You can become a better person by knowing how to read people. Reading people allows you to develop empathy. You can tell what others are feeling and respond accordingly. Your sensitivity will make you a more responsive and caring lover, parent, friend, and family member.

You can also protect yourself better from the harm of people with bad intentions. When you can read people, you are consequently able to spot people that will not benefit you. Before you get too far into a relationship of any nature with someone harmful, you can see what the person is about and prevent further harm from happening.

When it comes to choosing a good friend or lover, you are now better able to pick people that are good for your life. You can spot those that care for you and have the capability of treating you well. You can pick lovers and friends that have good track records.

CPSIA information can be obtained
at www.ICGtesting.com
Printed in the USA
BVHW092121090621
609098BV00002B/72